Grandma's Present

Written by Helen Depree

Illustrated by Bob Kerr

Dad and Sam and Tommy are in their new home.

Sam and Tommy are in bed.

"Thank you for helping me today,"
said Dad.
"You helped me get our new home
neat and clean."

"We liked helping you, Dad,"
said Sam and Tommy.
"And we like our new home."

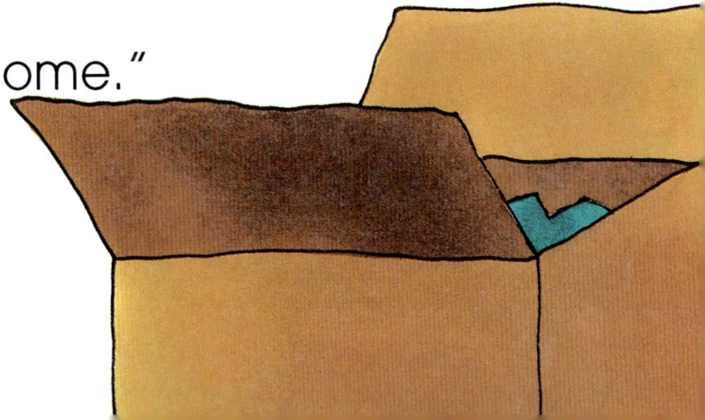

"Grandma helped us today, too," said Tommy.

"Can we get her a present for helping us?" said Sam.

The next day, Dad, Sam, and Tommy went to the garden shop.

They looked at all the plants.
"I like this one," said Sam.
"This is a good one."
Dad and Tommy liked it, too.

"Thank you for helping us, Grandma," said Dad.

"Here is a present for you," said Sam and Tommy. "It is for the garden."

"Thank you," said Grandma.

Grandma planted the plant
in her garden.
"Where are the flowers?" said Sharma.

"We will look after the plant,
and flowers will come," said Grandma.

Grandma watered the garden
day after day.
She looked at the plant on Monday,
Tuesday, Wednesday,
Thursday, and Friday.

On Saturday, it was Grandma's birthday.
"Grandma, come and look
in the garden!" shouted Jake.

"Happy birthday, Grandma!"